D1449015

PIONEERS

NATURE
LIFE & TIMES
AMERICAN GEOGRAPHY

Amanda Bennett

This book belongs to
_____

Pioneers:
Nature, Life & Times, American Geography

ISBN 1-888306-04-1

Copyright © 1996 by Amanda Bennett

Published by:
Homeschool Press
229 S. Bridge St.
P.O. Box 254
Elkton, MD 21922-0254

Send requests for information to the above address.

Cover design by Mark Dinsmore.

All rights reserved. No part of this publication may be reproduced, stored in a retrieval system, or transmitted in any form or by any means-electronic, mechanical, photocopy, recording, or any other-except for brief quotations in printed reviews, without the prior permission of the publisher. Pages containing the outline, unit questions and those designated for notes may be photocopied for use by the purchaser's own children.

Printed in the United States of America.

This book is dedicated to

grandparents everywhere, for taking the time to share

your love as well as your memories and dreams.

How To Use This Guide

Welcome to the world of unit studies! They present a wonderful method of learning for all ages and it is a great pleasure to share this unit study with you. This guide has been developed and written to provide a basic framework for the study, along with plenty of ideas and resources to help round out the learning adventure. All the research is done. These are READY to go!

TO BEGIN: The <u>Outline</u> is the study "skeleton", providing an overall view of the subject and important subtopics. It can be your starting point— read through it and familiarize yourself with the content. It is great for charting your course over the next few weeks (or developing lesson plans). Please understand that you do not necessarily have to proceed through the outline in order. I personally focus on the areas that our children are interested in first—giving them "ownership" of the study. By beginning with their interest areas, it gives us the opportunity to further develop these interests while stretching into other areas of the outline as they increase their topic knowledge.

By working on a unit study for five or six weeks at a time, you can catch the children's attention and hold it for valuable learning. I try to wrap up each unit study in five or six weeks, whether or not we have "completed" the unit outline. The areas of the outline that we did not yet cover may be covered the next time we delve into the unit study topic (in a few months or perhaps next year). These guides are <u>non-consumable</u>—you can use them over and over again, covering new areas of interest as you review the previous things learned in the process.

The <u>Reading and Reference Lists</u> are lists of resources that feed right into various areas of the <u>Outline</u>. The books are listed with grade level recommendations and all the information that you need to locate them in the library or from your favorite book retailer. You can also order them through the national Inter-Library Loan System (I.L.L.)—check with the reference librarian at your local library.

There are several other components that also support the unit study.

The <u>Spelling and Vocabulary Lists</u> identify words that apply directly to the unit study, and are broken down into both Upper and Lower Levels for use with several ages.

The <u>Suggested Software, Games and Videos Lists</u> includes games, software and videos that make the learning fun, while reinforcing some of the basic concepts studied.

The <u>Activities and Field Trip Lists</u> include specific activity materials and field trip ideas that can be used with this unit to give some hands-on learning experience.

The <u>Internet Resources List</u> identifies sites that you might find helpful with this unit. The Internet is a wonderful resource to use with unit studies providing the sights and sounds of things that you might never otherwise experience! You can see works of art in the Louvre. See the sunrise on Mt. Rushmore, hear the sounds of the seashore and find many other things that will help provide an "immersion" in the unit study topic, as never before, without ever leaving home. As with any resource, use it with care and be there with the students as they go exploring new learning opportunities.

The author and the publisher care about you and your family. While not all of the materials recommended in this guide are written from a Christian perspective, they all have great educational value. Please use caution when using any materials. It's important to take the time to review books, games, and Internet sites before your children use them to make sure they meet your family's expectations.

As you can see, all of these sections have been included to help you build your unit study into a fun and fruitful learning adventure. Unit studies provide an excellent learning tool and give the students lifelong memories about the topic and the study.

Lots of phone numbers and addresses have been included to assist you in locating specific books and resources. To the best of our knowledge, all of these numbers were correct at the time of printing.

The left-hand pages of this book have been left "almost" blank for your notes, resources, ideas, children's artwork, or diagrams from this study or for ideas that you might like to pursue the next time you venture into this unit.

"Have fun & Enjoy the Adventure!"

Table of Contents

Introduction

Remember the times that you spent playing make-believe pioneers or building forts in the backyard? What a thrill to try to build a fort from Dad's leftover lumber scraps, listen to all of the sounds of nature and try to move "like an Indian" through the underbrush without cracking a twig! Remember the smell of the rain, freshly-turned soil and honeysuckle in bloom? Many a child has spent countless hours at this kind of play in America. This study allows the same type of creativity while it focuses more closely on the details of the pioneer era in our country.

The lives of the pioneers were less complicated in many ways. They made do with what they had, observed the beauty of nature, and encountered adventure and challenge on a daily basis. They experienced a different pace of life. The most important things were the simplest things—food, water, shelter, sitting around the fire at night, reading the Bible together, sharing the day's excitements and difficulties and looking forward to Sunday for their hard-earned day of rest. There are many valuable lessons to be learned from these people and times.

This study covers the early expansion of our country, from the thirteen colonies to the massive move westward along the Oregon Trail. This era was an exciting and challenging time for America, for both the government and the people. Some of the topics covered include:

- Daily lives of the pioneers
- Nineteenth century American history
- Geography of the United States
- Science through nature
- North American Indians
- Transportation in early America

Let's travel with them now, feeling their heart's desire to seek freedom and adventure. Take your children along to see the sights through the eyes of the pioneers, the beauty and intensity of God's world, smell the campfires and taste the trail food and understand the excitement of finding their own "home place" at the end of the journey. Share these adventures with your children—let them savor those days and learn to appreciate the history of this country, "one nation, under God."

Study Outline

I. Introduction

A. The frontier of America changed as the new country grew
   1. Initially, the frontier was whatever was "outside" the thirteen colonies
   2. As more territories were added, the frontier lines moved and changed with each addition
   3. By the end of the nineteenth century, the frontiers were closing and pioneers had settled all across the continent
B. The efforts of the pioneers helped to make America a solid and unified country
C. The lessons to be learned from a study of pioneers are many
   1. Character qualities
      a. Faith
      b. Commitment
      c. Determination
      d. Courage
      e. Love
      f. Diligence
   2. Geography of the United States
   3. History of the United States during the late eighteenth and nineteenth century
   4. Transportation methods
   5. Daily life styles and family concepts
   6. Famous people involved in the pioneering efforts
   7. The Indians of North America

II. History

A. Reasons for going to new territories as pioneers
   1. Adventure
   2. Privacy
   3. Fertile land
   4. Freedom
   5. Economic gain
B. Early settlers
   1. Traveled on foot or by horse

2. Followed the trails left by animals

3. Sought a better life and economic conditions

C. Pioneers of the nineteenth century

1. Traveled on foot, by wagon, by boat and eventually by train

2. Followed the new trails, carved out by animals, Native Americans, and explorers

3. Sought more space, better land and improved economic conditions

III. Government Influence

A. The Northwest Ordinance of 1785 was passed by the Continental Congress to organize the surveying and sales of the land in the Northwest Territory (west of the original thirteen colonies, east of the Mississippi River and north of the Ohio River)

B. The Northwest Ordinance of 1787, set up the system of governing the Northwest Territory and defined the steps to statehood

C. The Constitution of the United States was signed in 1787

D. The Bill of Rights was written and became the first amendment to the Constitution in 1791

E. The Louisiana Purchase was completed in 1803 and doubled the size of the United States

F. In 1804, Lewis and Clark began their exploration of the west, sponsored by a $2.5 million expense budget from Congress

G. The Preemption Act in 1841 provided for squatters to purchase the land they occupied

H. The Homestead Act in 1862 provided for land to be obtained with the payment of a small fee and staying on the land for at least five years

IV. Major paths of travel in the days of the early pioneers

A. Forbes Road

B. Braddock's Road

C. Wilderness Trail

D. Cumberland Road

1. Construction began 1811

2. Created to cross the Allegheny Mountains

3. Connected Maryland and Illinois

E.   Oregon Trail
    1.   Originated in Missouri and ended in Oregon
    2.   Over 2,000 miles long
    3.   Followed several rivers west
    4.   Forts and other stops along the trail
       a.   Fort Kearney
       b.   Scott's Bluff
       c.   Chimney Rock
       d.   Fort Laramie
       e.   Independence Rock
       f.   Fort Bridger
       g.   Fort Hall
       h.   Fort Boise
       i.   Whitman Mission
       j.   Fort Vancouver

V.   Daily Life

A.   Life on the trail
    1.   Preparing for the journey
       a.   Planning for months in advance
       b.   Selecting what to pack and what to leave behind
       c.   Talking to others about any information available
    2.   Embarking on the long trip
       a.   Goodbyes to friends and family
       b.   The aches and pains of travel
       c.   Finding food along the way
          (1)   Supplies brought from the outset were used first
          (2)   Hunting wildlife on the trail
             (a)   Deer
             (b)   Buffalo
             (c)   Rabbit
             (d)   Bear
             (e)   Squirrel
             (f)   Prairie Dog
             (g)   Raccoon
             (h)   Antelope

        d. The sights and sounds of the trip
          (1) Landmarks
          (2) Other travelers
          (3) Wildlife
          (4) Weather over the seasons of the journey
          (5) Births, deaths and illness
        e. Stops along the way
          (1) Sundays were days to stop, worship and rest
          (2) River crossings
          (3) Chimney Rock
          (4) Independence Rock
          (5) Forts built along the route to provide provisions and a resting place before the next part of the journey

B. Life in the new home
    1. Clearing the land needed for the home
    2. Building the home
        a. First lodging at the homesite was usually temporary (shack, shanty or dugout)
        b. Permanent lodging was built later
          (1) Log cabin construction if there were readily-available trees
          (2) Sod construction if the home was built on the prairie
    3. Daily chores
        a. Cooking
        b. Cleaning
        c. Tending the livestock
        d. Planting, tending and harvesting crops
        e. Maintaining the homestead, outbuildings, and fences
        f. Fetching water
        g. Collecting and chopping firewood
        h. Making, washing and mending clothes
        i. Watching the younger children

C. Entertainment
    1. Music
        a. Singing of hymns, wagon train songs and classic settler songs

b.   Instruments for accompaniment
       (1)   Fiddle
       (2)   Banjo
       (3)   Harmonica (mouth organ)

2.   Social life

     a.   Church or Sunday get-togethers for worship

     b.   Quilting bees

     c.   Corn huskings

     d.   House and barn raisings

VI.   Transportation

A.   Walking

     1.   On early trails that were too narrow for a wagon

     2.   Beside the wagons along the later trails

B.   Riding

     1.   Horse

     2.   Mule

C.   Wagon

     1.   Prairie schooner

     2.   Conestoga wagon

D.   Boat

     1.   Canoe

     2.   Steamboat

     3.   Canal boat and barge

E.   Train

VII.   Famous people in the pioneering of America

A.   Thomas Jefferson

B.   Meriwether Lewis

C.   William Clark

D.   Sacajawea

E.   Marcus Whitman, M.D.

F.   Narcissa Whitman

G.   John Chapman (Johnny Appleseed)

H.   Kit Carson

I   Daniel Boone

J.   Davy Crockett

K. Zebulon Pike
L. Buffalo Bill
M. Jedediah Smith

VIII. North American Indians

A. Tribal regions
1. Northeast
2. Southeast
3. Plains
4. California
5. Basin
6. Plateau
7. Northwest
8. Southwest
B. Tribes of the Plains region of the pioneer travels
1. Apache
2. Blackfoot
3. Cheyenne
4. Comanche
5. Crow
6. Dakota
7. Iowa
8. Pawnee
9. Shoshoni
10. Sioux
C. Each tribe was unique in their beliefs and daily lives and habits
1. Basic beliefs
2. Daily life
   a. Family responsibilities
   b. Shelter
   c. Food
   d. Children and their roles
3. Tribal philosophies toward the pioneers
D. Indian issues with the pioneers and American government
1. Unkept agreements
2. Killing and destruction of their food sources
3. Introduction of new diseases, like measles and cholera

IX.   Science in the life of the pioneers

    A.   Survival skills
        1.   Ability to find food
        2.   Ability to find water
        3.   Maintain good health
        4.   Care for those afflicted with illness or wounds
    B.   Tracking and observation skills
        1.   To find food
        2.   To follow the trail of others
    C.   Wayfinding skills
        1.   Knowledge of the anticipated trail
        2.   Ability to determine direction using the sun and moon and stars
        3.   Observing nature for other obvious directions
    D.   Inventions that impacted the pioneering efforts
        1.   Barbed wire
        2.   Telegraph
        3.   Photography
        4.   Improved farming tools

X.   Classic literature

    A.   *The Little House Series* of books by Laura Ingalls Wilder
    B.   *The Adventures of Tom Sawyer* and *The Adventures of Huckleberry Finn* by Mark Twain (Samuel Clemens)
    C.   *The Oregon Trail* by Francis Parkman
    D.   *The Last of the Mohicans* by James Fenimore Cooper

Spelling/Vocabulary List

Lower Level

pack	sew
home	mend
trail	fix
pans	dog
wagon	cook
wheel	flour
walk	beans
shoes	mush
hat	corn
pray	meal
oxen	circle
horse	sod
mule	grass
yoke	fire
feed	wood
cow	Bible
hen	rifle
pot	flint
hunt	Indian
travel	kettle
dust	raid
rain	bow
wind	arrow
snow	friend
sun	promise
heat	team
cold	fort
breeze	find
dry	pass
chill	bread

Spelling/Vocabulary List

Upper Level

challenge
seeking
traveler
homesteader
trapper

mountain
barter
daylight
landmark
compass

survive
supplies
tools
repair
responsibility

wisdom
drought
determination
commitment
nature

industrious
scenery
continent
overland
route

commerce
destination
speculate
dugout
soddy

quilt
trapping
buckskin
gunpowder
claim

stake
locust
railroad
medicine
missionary

frontier
independence
expansion
measles
cholera

buffalo
rattlesnake
badger
sage hen
rabbit

coyote
wolves
raccoon
bison
venison

Oregon
Santa Fe
California
Missouri
Dakota

Writing Ideas

Here are some ideas to help incorporate writing in a unit study. Choose one or two and watch what happens!

1. This study provides a wonderful opportunity to study first-hand accounts of other people's lives through their diaries and journals. Books like those by Laura Ingalls Wilder, ***A Gathering of Days: A New England Girl's Journal, 1830 - 1832, Diary of an Early American Boy*** and others provide this perspective. After reading some of these, have your child begin to write or dictate their own daily journal during the unit study, or on an upcoming trip or other adventure.

2. If your child is interested in the Little House series of books, have him write a letter requesting information about Laura Ingalls Wilder and museum locations, books, etc., and address the letter to:

    > Laura Ingalls Wilder Home and Museum
    > 3068 Highway A
    > Mansfield, MO 65704

    When he writes, have him include a long, self-addressed stamped envelope. This is the address for the actual house that Laura and Almanzo lived in and where the Little House books were written, their Rocky Ridge Farm.

3. To help foster their creativity, consider having your students develop their own tale about life on the wagon trail or life on the prairie. One of the things that you will notice as you study this topic with your children is that the simplest things for daily living were vital for the survival of a pioneering family—things like fresh water, a food supply, shelter and safety. While we tend to take these things for granted, the pioneers didn't have that luxury. Writing/dictating a story about one day in the life of a pioneer child (his responsibilities, family life and what he might have experienced in a typical day) will help your child get a clearer picture of the work as well as the importance of family to a child of the pioneers. To get him started, read one of the books about the life of a pioneer child with him (A Pioneer Sampler: The Daily Life of a Pioneer Family in 1840, If You Traveled West in a Covered Wagon or any of the other resources listed in the Reference Resources - Daily Life Section of this guide).

4. A study of the pioneers would not be complete without studying the rich and plentiful supply of real pioneers. Have your student select one of the famous pioneers to study, reading biographies and other accounts of their lives. Then, interview your student as they "roleplay" this character, asking about their past, their family, and other adventures they experienced along the trail. Write down their responses as they develop their story, or have the older student write down their responses to your written questions. If you have more than one student, let them interview each other as they "roleplay" different pioneers.

Activity Ideas

Activities provide a great way to reinforce the material that we learn in a unit study. This supplies important hands-on learning while we have fun and are challenged at the same time. There are activity books available about the pioneers, westward expansion and nature at most libraries, and your family will probably come up with some fun activities of their own.

As we work on a unit, we use activity materials like those listed in the **Activity Resources**, as well as some of our own ideas. Here are a few activity ideas to get you started, and don't be surprised if the children come up with some great ones on their own!

1. Pioneer children had to walk at least ten miles in an average day. To give the children a feel for just how far this is, plan a hike of several miles and clock it in your car first. Then, take the hike with them. Take along a snack or picnic lunch. Discuss things like the plants and animals you see, and how the pioneers had to walk five times as far as this, etc. Tired feet and sore muscles will help them really appreciate just how hard life on the trail could be!

2. Plan a "pioneer" type of day or evening outside. Take advantage of some of the everyday things that can be done outside to get a taste of "roughing" it. Plan to cook outside, collect and sketch some of the local plants and animal life, work in the garden, etc. If possible, turn this event into an outdoor camping adventure. You will see the night life as well as the daytime events when staying outdoors. Make sure you photograph the day's events—you should see the photo of the first baked potato "briquettes" I ever tried to cook in the coals of a fire!

3. If your children have any interest in basic carpentry, this study lends itself well to learning about the basics. The children can try a hand at some simple furniture construction. If you are uncomfortable with trying to build something simple from scratch, write or call The Carpenter's Son Woodcraft, 3209 Willowbrook Circle, Waco, TX 76711. (817) 756-5261. Request a copy of their free catalog—they carry quite a selection of simple kits for even younger children to assemble, and the results are quite impressive.

4.	Quiltmaking also goes hand-in-hand with this unit study. Check out some of the resources listed in the **Activities Resources** section, and look in the children's section of your library for beginning books on quilting. If you have a huge pile of scraps and rags, or even some old clothes hanging around, cut some simple pieces for your student's beginning quilting efforts.

Activity Resources

Tasha Tudor's Old Fashioned Gifts: Presents and Favors for All Occasions,
by Tasha Tudor and Linda Allen. Published by David McKay Co., subsidiary
of Random House Books, 400 Hahn Rd., Westminster, MD 21157.
(800) 733-3000.

***The Little House Cookbook: Frontier Foods from Laura Ingalls Wilder's
Classic Stories,*** by Barbara M. Walker. Grades 4 and up. Published by Harper
& Row, 10 E. 53rd St., New York, NY 10022. (212) 207-7000.

My Book of Little House Paper Dolls, by Renee Graef. Grades Pre-K-5.
Published by HarperCollins Children's Books, 1000 Keystone Industrial Park,
Scranton, PA 18512. (800) 242-7737. Available from Farm Country General
Store, Rte. 1 Box 63, Metamora, IL 61548. (800) 551-FARM.

Drawing From Nature and ***Drawing Life in Motion,*** by Jim Arnosky. Grades 5
and up. Published by Lothrop, Lee & Shepard Books, a division of William
Morrow & Company, 39 Plymouth St., Fairfield, NJ 07004. (800) 843-9389.

***The Local Wilderness: Observing Neighborhood Nature Through An Artist's
Eye,*** by Cathy Johnson. Grades 7-12. Published by Prentice Hall Press, a division of Simon & Schuster, 200 Old Tappan Rd., Old Tappan, NJ 07675.
(800) 223-2348.

***Kirsten's Cookbook: A Peek at Dining in the Past with Meals You Can Cook
Today,*** The American Girls Collection. Published by Pleasant Company
Publications, Inc., P.O. Box 620998, Middleton, WI 53562.
(800) 845-0005.

Nature Crafts Workshop, by Will Kirkman. Grades 4-8. Published by Fearon
Teacher Aids, P.O. Box 280, Carthage, IL 62321.

The Quilt-Block History of Pioneer Days: With Projects Kids Can Make, by
Mary Cobb. Grades 2-4. Published by The Millbrook Press, 2 Old New
Milford Rd., Brookfield, CT 06804-0335. (800) 462-4703.

My Grandmother's Patchwork Quilt: A Book & Pocketful of Patchwork Pieces, by Jane Bolton. Grades 3 and up. Published by Bantam, Doubleday, Dell., Consumer Services, P.O. Box 507, Des Plains, IL 60017. (800) 223-6834. Available from Farm Country General Store, Rte. 1, Box 63, Metamora, IL 61548. (800) 551-3276.

More Than Moccasins: A Kid's Activity Guide to Traditional North American Indian Life, by Laurie Carlson. Grades Pre-K-5. Published by Chicago Review Press. Distributed by: Independent Publishers Group, 814 N. Franklin Street, Chicago, IL 60610. (800) 888-4741.

Finger Weaving: Indian Braiding, by Alta R. Turner. Published by Cherokee Publications, P.O. Box 256, Cherokee, NC 28719.

Do People Grow On Family Trees? Genealogy for Kids & Other Beginners, by Ira Wolfman. Grades 5-12. Published by Workman Publishing Company, 708 Broadway, New York, NY 10003.

Pioneers: An Educational Coloring Book, by Linda Spizziri. Grades 1-8. Published by Spizziri Publishing Company, P.O. Box 9397, Rapid City, SD 57709. (605) 348-2749.

Coloring books from Dover Publishing, 31 East 2nd Street, Mineola, NY 11501. Great for Grades 3 and up:
> ***Lewis & Clark Expedition***
> ***American Wildflowers***
> ***Old Fashioned Farm Life***
> ***Indian Tribes of North America***

Maps & Mazes: A First Guide to Mapmaking, by Gillian Chapman and Pam Robson. Grades 2-4. Published by The Millbrook Press, 2 Old New Milford Rd., Brookfield, CT 06804-0335. (800) 462-4703.

Draw 50 Animals, by Lee J. Ames. Grades 5-12. Published by Doubleday, a division of Bantam Doubleday Dell Publishing Group, 2451 South Wolf Rd., Des Plains, IL 60018. (800) 323-9872.

Job Opportunities

Here is a list of jobs that involve some of the aspects of pioneer life and adventures. There are others that I'm sure you will identify, but these are some of the main ones that we investigated during our unit study.

Historian	Wildlife management
Botanist	Museum curator
Biologist	Historical interpreter
Farmer	Groundskeeper/manager
Agricultural engineer	Building construction
County extension agent	Carpenter
Landscape architect	Veterinarian
Plant taxonomist	Missionary
Horticulturalist scientist	Soil scientist
Forest ranger	Nursery worker/owner
Entomologist	Gardener
Mining engineer	Geologist
Wilderness guide	Rancher

For more information about these jobs or others that may be interesting, go to the reference librarian in the public library and ask for publications on careers. Some that we recommend are:

The Encyclopedia of Careers and Vocational Guidance, published by J. G. Ferguson Publishing Company, Chicago.

Occupational Outlook Handbook, published by the U.S. Department of Labor, Bureau of Labor Statistics. It presents detailed information on the 250 occupations that employ the vast majority of workers. It describes the nature of work, training and educational requirements, working conditions and earnings potential.

Games, Videos and Software

Games are a great way to reinforce the material that we learn. We have fun while reviewing important information and concepts around the kitchen table or on the computer. The software listed here is just a small sample of what is available. During the writing of this book, several new games and software packages are in development for release in the near future, and all sound very exciting! Check around at your local toy and software stores to find out the latest introductions.

Software:

There are several versions of a fun and educational software game, **The Oregon Trail,** available as this book goes to press. It is published by MECC, 6160 Summit Dr. N., Minneapolis, MN 55430. (800) 685-MECC.

Games:

Made For Trade, a board game focusing on early American daily life, trading and bartering, and history. Grades 3 and up. Published by Aristoplay, P.O. Box 7529, Ann Arbor, MI 48107. (800) 634-7738.

Herd Your Horses, a board game about horses that is fun for Grades 3 and up. Published by Aristoplay, P.O. Box 7529, Ann Arbor, MI 48107. (800) 634-7738.

Videos:

There are many, many videos available, for purchase or on loan from your local library, about all kinds of pioneers, and some of our favorites are the classics:

Little House on the Prairie (there are several full length special videos available)

Sarah, Plain and Tall

Old Yeller

Field Trip Ideas

There are so many field trips that your family can enjoy while they learn about pioneers. It is hard to list all of the ones that you might want to consider. Please use this list to get started planning some field trips, then let your imagination identify others that may be in your area. Don't forget to take along your camera to capture some of the sights of the surroundings as well as the children! Also, remember to write the places that you visit and thank them for their time, or have one of the older children do the note-writing.

1. If your child is interested in the Little House series of books, consider taking a field trip to one of the Little House sites and museums. To get a list of all the museum locations, write:

    Laura Ingalls Wilder Home and Museum
    3068 Highway A
    Mansfield, MO 65704

    When you write, include a long, self-addressed stamped envelope. This is the address for the actual house that Laura and Almanzo lived in and where the Little House books were written, their Rocky Ridge Farm. It is open to the public for viewing, and makes for a wonderful and memorable field trip or travel stop during a vacation. You can see the original manuscripts that Laura Ingalls Wilder wrote for some of the Little House books. If you would like to call the museum and bookstore, their phone number is (417) 924-3626.

2. While studying pioneers, consider visiting some of the early pioneer sites or buildings in your area or state. There are usually several museums maintained by the state that house artifacts and documents of the early settlers to your area. They provide some valuable insight to just how close the real "pioneers" of America were to your own hometown.

3. In some areas of the country, there are "living history" museums or re-enactments where people portray settlers or characters of a certain time period. These are great field trips to attend, and the children get the chance to question these people first-hand! Look for those that are about pioneers, Native Americans, wagon trains, etc.

4.   Many local libraries maintain old copies of the local newspaper, as well as many other "archive" materials that pertain to the history of your area. You might have to ask the reference librarian for help in locating some of these items, but the search is usually well worth the effort. The old photos and newspaper articles are interesting to older children, and they will begin to recognize some of the people's names and relate them to local landmarks, statues and street or bridge names. It is an interesting way to become familiar with local history, as well as the various resources of the library.

Subject Search Words

This list of **SUBJECT** search words has been included to help you with this unit study. To find material about pioneers and other related topics, go to the card catalog or computerized holdings catalog in your library and look up:

General:

Pioneers
Settlers
Frontier
Wilderness
Cumberland Gap
Cumberland Road
Wilderness Road
Oregon Trail
Santa Fe Trail
Covered wagon
Conestoga wagon
Wagon train
Prairie schooner
Willamette Valley
Lewis and Clark
Westward expansion
Prairie life
Prairie
Pioneer life
Pony Express
Soddy
Buffalo
Fur trade
American exploration
Quilts/quilting
Appalachia
Chimney Rock
Independence Rock
Continental Divide

People:

Thomas Jefferson
Daniel Boone
Davy Crockett
Marcus Whitman, M.D.
Narcissa Whitman
Kit Carson
Meriwether Lewis
William Clark
Zebulon Pike
Sacajawea
Johnny Appleseed
Robert Fulton
Samuel Morse
John Deere

Miscellaneous:

Louisiana Purchase
Homestead Act
Northwest Ordinance of 1785
Railroad Act
Pre-Emption Act
Erie Canal
Pony Express

Trivia Questions

These questions have been included for fun and will reinforce some of the material that you might read during this study. Enjoy the search for answers, and then compare them with the answers that we found, located on the page 57.

1. Where did the name "Conestoga" come from when referring to a Conestoga wagon?

2. Where did Independence Rock get its name?

3. Which President was the first to take the oath of office in Washington, D.C.?

4. What was the first real "trail" through the Appalachian Mountains?

5. Wagon trains headed out on the Oregon Trail usually assembled and began their journey from what town?

6. How many months did it usually take to travel the Oregon Trail, from Missouri to Oregon?

7. What flag flew over the fort at the end of the Oregon Trail during the first few years?

8. What tool did John Deere help re-design in 1838 that made it easier to "harvest" sod for a soddy?

9. What was the first message sent by Samuel Morse over the telegraph?

Trivia Answers

1. Where did the name "Conestoga" come from when referring to a Conestoga wagon?

    From the town where the wagons were originally built, Conestoga, Pennsylvania.

2. Where did Independence Rock get its name?

    The settlers tried to reach this landmark slab of granite by the Fourth of July, Independence Day. They wanted to reach this landmark by Independence Day if they had any hope of reaching the end of the Oregon Trail before the onset of winter.

3. Which President was the first to take the oath of office in Washington, D.C.?

    Thomas Jefferson, in 1801

4. What was the first real "trail" through the Appalachian Mountains?

    The Cumberland Gap

5. Wagon trains headed out on the Oregon Trail usually assembled and began their journey from what town?

    Independence, Missouri

6. How many months did it usually take to travel the Oregon Trail, from Missouri to Oregon?

    It took five to six months, on the average.

7. What flag flew over the fort at the end of the Oregon Trail during the first few years?

    The Union Jack of Great Britain

8. What tool did John Deere help re-design in 1838 that made it easier to "harvest" sod for a soddy?

    The plow

9. What was the first message sent by Samuel Morse over the telegraph?

    "What hath God wrought"

Reference Resources
History

Pioneers, by Dennis B. Fradin. (A New True Book). Grades K-3. Published by Children's Press, P.O. Box 1331, Danbury, CT 06813. (800) 621-1115.

Settling the American West, by Jim Collins. Grades Pre-K-3. (First Books Series). Published by Franklin Watts, 5450 Cumberland Ave., Chicago, IL 60656. (800) 672-6672.

Pioneers: A Library of Congress Book, by Martin W. Sandler. Grades 5 and up. Published by HarperCollins Children's Books, 1000 Keystone Industrial Park, Scranton, PA 18512. (800) 242-7737.

From Sea to Shining Sea for Children, by Peter Marshall and Anna Fishel. Grades 5 and up. Published by Fleming H. Revell, a division of Baker Book House Company, P.O. Box 6287, Grand Rapids, MI 49516-6287.

Daniel Boone and the Wilderness Road, by Catherine E. Chambers. Grades 5-9. (Adventures in Frontier America Series). Published by Troll Associates, 100 Corporate Dr., Mahwah, NJ 07430. (800) 526-5289.

Daniel Boone and the Opening of the Ohio Country, by Seamus Cavan. (World Explorer Series). Grades 5 and up. Published by Chelsea House, 1974 Sproul Rd., Suite 400, P.O. Box 914, Broomall, PA 19008. (800) 848-2665.

Cumberland Gap and Trails West, by Edith S. McCall. (Frontiers of America Series). Grades 3-8. © 1961. Published by Children's Press, P.O. Box 1331, Danbury, CT 06813. (800) 621-1115. This is an older book, but describes the adventures of men like George Washington and Daniel Boone as they explored the Appalachian Mountains and opened new trails to the West.

Wagons Over the Mountains, by Edith S. McCall. (Frontiers of America Series). Grades 3-8. © 1961. Published by Children's Press, P.O. Box 1331, Danbury, CT 06813. (800) 621-1115. This is an older book, but contains true stories about real people as they traveled from Philadelphia to Pittsburgh, as well as other wagon adventures as the frontier moved westward.

Bold Journey: West With Lewis and Clark, by Charles Bohner. Grades 5 and up. Published by Houghton Mifflin Co., Individual/Trade Division, 181 Ballardvale Rd., Wilmington, MA 01887 (800) 225-3362/School Division, 1900 Batavia Ave., Geneva, IL 60134 (800) 323-5663.

The Story of the Great American West, Published by Reader's Digest Association, Customer Service, Readers Digest Rd., Pleasantville, NY 10570. (800) 431-1246.

The Advancing Frontier, by Trudy Hamner. (Issues in American History Series). Grades 7 and up. Published by Franklin Watts, 5450 Cumberland Ave., Chicago, IL 60656. (800) 672-6672.

Bridging the Continent, The Conquest of the West, Exploring the Frontier, Native Americans of the West and **The Riches of the West,** all from the Sourcebooks on the American West, part of the American Albums from the Collections of the Library of Congress. Grades 5-8. Published by The Millbrook Press, 2 Old New Milford Rd., Brookfield, CT 06804-0335. (800) 462-4703.

Frontier Living, by Edwin Tunis. Grades 7 and up. Published by HarperCollins Children's Books, 1000 Keystone Industrial Park, Scranton, PA 18512. (800) 242-7737.

If You Traveled West in a Covered Wagon, by Ellen Levine. Grades 3-5. Published by Scholastic, Inc., P.O. Box 7502, Jefferson City, MO 65102. (800) 325-6149.

Going West: Cowboys and Pioneers, by Martine Courtault. Grades K-5. (Young Discovery Library Series). Published by Young Discovery Library.

The Pioneers, by Huston Horn. (The Old West Series). Grades 6-12. Published by Time-Life Books. ©1974. This is a wonderful addition to a study of pioneers with plenty of paintings and photographs of the pioneers and their trails and leaders.

The Transcontinental Railroad: Triumph of a Dream, by Dan Elish. (Spotlight on American History). Grades 4-6. Published by The Millbrook Press, 2 Old New Milford Rd., Brookfield, CT 06804-0335. (800) 462-4703.

Reference Resources
Adventures

Wagons West: Off to Oregon, by Catherine Chambers. Grades 5-9. (Adventures in Frontier America Series). Grades 4-6. Published by Troll Associates, 100 Corporate Dr., Mahwah, NJ 07430. (800) 526-5289.

Oregon Trail, by Leonard Fisher. Grades 3-7. Published by Holiday House, 425 Madison Ave., New York, NY 10017. (212) 688-0085.

A Pioneer Sampler: The Daily Life of a Pioneer Family in 1840, by Barbara Greenwood. Grades 4-12. Published by Ticknor & Fields Books for Young Readers, a Houghton Mifflin Company, Industrial/Trade Division, 181 Ballardvale Rd., Wilmington, MA 01887 (800) 225-3362/School Division, 1900 Batavia Ave., Geneva, IL 60134 (800) 323-5663.

The Prairie Traveler: The Classic Handbook for American Pioneers, by Randolph Marcy, Captain, U.S. Army. Grades 7-12. First published in 1859 at the request of the U.S. War Department, this is a reprint of the guide many settlers used as a handbook for their westward journeys. Published by Perigree Books, The Putnam Berkeley Group, 390 Murray Hill Parkway, East Rutherford, NJ 07073. (800) 631-8571.

Growing Up in America: 1830-1860, by Evelyn Toynton. Grades 4-6. Published by The Millbrook Press, 2 Old New Milford Rd., Brookfield, CT 06804-0335. (800) 462-4703.

Frontier Home, by Raymond Bial. Grades K-5. Published by Houghton Mifflin Co., Individual/Trade Division, 181 Ballardvale Rd., Wilmington, MA 018887 (800) 225-3362/Schools Division, 1900 Batavia Ave., Geneva, IL 60134 (800) 323-5663.

The Story of Women Who Shaped the West, by Mary Virginia Fox. (Cornerstones of Freedom Series). Grades 3-6. Published by Children's Press, P.O. Box 1331, Danbury, CT 06813. (800) 621-1115.

If You're Not From the Prairie..., by David Bouchard. Published by Simon & Schuster Trade, 200 Old Tappan Rd., Old Tappan, NJ 07675. (800) 223-2348.

Reference Resources
North American Indians

If You Lived With the Sioux Indians. Grades K -3. Published by Scholastic, Inc., P.O. Box 7502, Jefferson City, MO 65102. (800) 325-6149.

The Very First Americans, by Cara Ashrose. (All Aboard Books). Grades Pre-K-3. Published by Putnam Berkeley Group, 390 Murray Hill Parkway, East Rutherford, NJ 07073. (800) 631-8571.

More Than Moccasins: A Kid's Activity Guide to Traditional North American Indian Life, by Laurie Carlson. Grades Pre-K-5. Published by Chicago Review Press. Distributed by: Independent Publishers Group, 814 N. Franklin Street, Chicago, IL 60610. (800) 888-4741.

Finger Weaving: Indian Braiding, by Alta R. Turner. Published by Cherokee Publications, P.O. Box 256, Cherokee, NC 28719.

The How and Why Wonder Book of North American Indians, by Felix Sutton. Grades 2-8. Published by Price Stern Sloan, 360 N. La Cienega Boulevard, Los Angeles, CA 90048. (800) 421-0892.

I Can Read About Indians, by Elizabeth Warren. Grades Pre-K-2. Published by Troll Associates, 100 Corporate Dr., Mahwah, NJ 07430. (800) 526-5289.

Reference Resources
Transportation

The Amazing Impossible Erie Canal, by Cheryl Harness. Grades K-6.
Published by Simon & Schuster, 200 Old Tappan Rd., Old Tappan, NJ 07675.
(800) 223-2348.

Early Travel, by Bobbie Kalman. Grades 3-6. (Early Settler Life Series).
Published by Crabtree Publishing, 350 Fifth Avenue, Suite 3308, New York,
NY 10118. (800) 387-7650.

Pioneers on Early Waterways: Davy Crockett and Mark Twain, by Edith S.
McCall. (Frontiers of America Series). Published by Children's Press, P.O. Box
1331, Danbury, CT 06813. (800) 621-1115.

If You Traveled West in a Covered Wagon, by Ellen Levine. Grades 3-5.
Published by Scholastic, Inc., P.O. Box 7502, Jefferson City, MO 65102.
(800) 325-6149.

Daily Life in a Covered Wagon, by Paul Erickson. Grades 3 and up. Published
by Preservation Press, 1785 Massachusetts Ave N.W., Washington, DC 20036.
(800) 766-6847.

The Prairie Schooners, by Glen Rounds. Grades 4-12. Published by Holiday
House, 425 Madison Ave., New York, NY 10017. (212) 688-0085. ©1968.

Pony Express, by Laurel Van der Linde. Grades 6 and up. Published by Simon
& Schuster, 200 Old Tappan Rd., Old Tappan, NJ 07675.
(800) 223-2348.

Pony Express: Hoofbeats in the Wilderness, by Joseph DiCerto. Grades 3-5.
Published by Franklin Watts, 5450 Cumberland Ave., Chicago, IL 60656.
(800) 672-6672.

The Transcontinental Railroad: Triumph of a Dream, by Dan Elish.
(Spotlight on American History). Grades 4-6. Published by The Millbrook
Press, 2 Old New Milford Rd., Brookfield, CT 06804-0335. (800) 462-4703.

Reference Resources
Everyday Life

Huskings, Quiltings, & Barn Raisings: Work-Play Parties in Early America, by Victoria Sherrow. Grades 3 and up. Published by Walker & Company, 435 Hudson St., New York, NY 10014. (800) 289-2553.

The Gristmill, Home Crafts, The Kitchen, Tools and Gadgets, A Child's Day and Settler Sayings, all written by Bobbie Kalman. Grades K-8. (Historic Community Series). Published by Crabtree Publishing, 350 Fifth Avenue, Suite 3308, New York, NY 10118. (800) 387-7650.

The Early Family Home, Early Settler Children, Early Christmas, Food For the Settler, all written by Bobbie Kalman. Grades K-8. (Early Settler Life Series). Published by Crabtree Publishing, 350 Fifth Avenue, Suite 3308, New York, NY 10118. (800) 387-7650.

Early Farm Life, by Lise Gunby. Grades 3-4. (Early Settler Series). Published by Crabtree Publishing, 350 Fifth Avenue, Suite 3308, New York, NY 10118. (800) 387-7650.

To Be a Pioneer, by Paul C. Burns and Ruth Hines. Grades 4 and up. Published by Abingdon Press, ©1962. Excellent resource for insight into the daily lives and adventures of the pioneers.

How the Settlers Lived, by George & Ellen Laycock. Grades 4 and up. Published by David McKay & Co., subsidiary of Random House Books, 400 Hahn Rd., Westminster, MD 21157. (800) 733-3000.

Log Cabin Home: Pioneers in the Wilderness, by Catherine E. Chambers. Grades 5-9. (Adventures in Frontier America Series) . Published by Troll Associates, 100 Corporate Dr., Mahwah, NJ 07430. (800) 526-5289.

Log Cabin in the Woods: A True Story About a Pioneer Boy, by Joanne Henry. Grades 2-5. Published by Simon & Schuster Children's, 200 Old Tappan Rd., Old Tappan, NJ 07675. (800) 223-2348.

Sod Houses on the Great Plains, by Glen Rounds. Grades 3 and up. Published by Holiday House, 425 Madison Ave., New York, NY 10017. (212) 688-0085.

Sod Walls: The Story of the Nebraska Sod House, by Roger L. Welsch. Grades 7-12. Published by Purcells, Inc., Broken Bow, Nebraska. ©1968. This is a very detailed book about the construction of sod houses during the 1800's. It has some of the first pioneer photographs taken on the prairies.

Reference Resources
Famous People

CHILDHOOD OF FAMOUS AMERICAN SERIES:
Davy Crockett: Young Rifleman, by Aileen W. Parks,
Daniel Boone: Young Hunter & Tracker, by Augusta Stevenson,
Mark Twain: Young Writer, by Miriam E. Mason and
Buffalo Bill: Frontier Daredevil, by Augusta Stevenson. Grades 2-6. Published by Aladdin Paperbacks, Simon & Schuster Children's Publishing Division, 200 Old Tappan Rd., Old Tappan, NJ 07675. (800) 223-2348.

Daniel Boone: Frontier Adventures, by Keith Brandt. Grades 4-6. Published by Troll Associates, 100 Corporate Dr., Mahwah, NJ 07430. (800) 526-5289.

Davy Crockett: Young Pioneer, by Laurence Santrey. Grades 4-6. Published by Troll Associates, 100 Corporate Dr., Mahwah, NJ 07430.
(800) 526-5289.

Kit Carson, by Jan Gleiter & Kathleen Thompson. Grades 2-6. (First Biographies Series). Published by Raintree Steck-Vaughn, P.O. Box 26015, Austin, TX 78755. (800) 531-5015.

Kit Carson: Pathfinder of the West, by Nardi R. Campion. Grades 2-6. (Discovery Biography Series). Published by Chelsea House, 1974 Sproul Rd., Suite 400, P.O. Box 914, Broomall, PA 19008. (800) 848-2665.

Johnny Appleseed-John Chapman: God's Faithful Planter, by David R. Collins. (The Sower Series) Grades 5 and up. Published by Mott Media, 1000 E. Huron, Milford, MI 48381. (810) 685-8773.

ROOKIE BIOGRAPHY SERIES:
John Chapman: The Man Who was Johnny Appleseed,
Daniel Boone: Man of the Forests,
Mark Twain: Author of Tom Sawyer and
Laura Ingalls Wilder: Author of the Little House Books, all by Carol Green. Grades K-3. Published by Children's Press, P.O. Box 1331, Danbury, CT 06813. (800) 621-1115.

Narcissa Whitman: Pioneer of Oregon, by Jeanette Eaton. Grades 7 and up. Published by Harcourt, Brace & World, New York. Copyright 1941—this is an older book, but has a refreshing perspective on the work of these dedicated missionaries on the Oregon Trail.

If You Grew Up With Abraham Lincoln, by Ann McGovern. Grades 3-5. Published by Scholastic, Inc., P.O. Box 7502, Jefferson City, MO 65102. (800) 325-6149.

Samuel Morse, by Mona Kerby. Grades 3-5. Published by Franklin Watts, 5450 Cumberland Ave., Chicago, IL 60656. (800) 672-6672.

Laura Ingalls Wilder, by William Anderson. Grades 3-7. Published by HarperCollins Children's Books, 1000 Keystone Industrial Pike, Scranton, PA 18512. (800) 242-7737.

Laura Ingalls Wilder: Author of the Little House Books, by Carol Greene. (Rookie Biography Series). Grades K-3. Published by Children's Press, P.O. Box 1331, Danbury, CT 06813. (800) 621-1115.

Pioneers on Early Waterways: Davy Crockett and Mark Twain, by Edith S. McCall. (Frontiers of America Series). Published by Children's Press, P.O. Box 1331, Danbury, CT 06813. (800) 621-1115.

Jedediah Smith and the Mountain Men of the American West, by John L. Allen. (World Explorer Series) Grades 5 and up. Published by Chelsea House, 1974 Sproul Rd., Suite 400, P.O. Box 914, Broomall, PA 19008. (800) 848-2665.

Reference Resources
Laura Ingalls Wilder

Laura Ingalls Wilder, by William Anderson. Grades 3-7. Published by HarperCollins Children's Books, 1000 Keystone Industrial Park, Scranton, PA 18512. (800) 242-7737.

Searching for Laura Ingalls: A Readers Journal, by Kathryn Knight and Meribah Knight. Grades 2-6. Published by Simon & Schuster Children's Books, 200 Old Tappan Rd., Old Tappan, NJ 07675. (800) 223-2348.

Laura Ingalls Wilder: Author of the Little House Books, by Carol Greene. (Rookie Biography Series). Grades K-3. Published by Children's Press, P.O. Box 1331, Danbury, CT 06813. (800) 621-1115.

On The Way Home: The Diary of a Trip From South Dakota to Mansfield, Missouri, in 1894, by Laura Ingalls Wilder. Grades 6-10. Published by HarperCollins Children's Books, 1000 Keystone Industrial Park, Scranton, PA 18512. (800) 242-7737.

Little House Country: A Photo Guide to the Homesites of Laura Ingalls Wilder, by William Anderson and Leslie Kelly. Grades K-6. Published by Anderson Publications, Box 423, Davison, MI 48423. (313) 667-2012.

Laura Ingalls Wilder Country: The People and Places in Laura Ingalls Wilder's Life and Books, by William Anderson. Published by HarperCollins, 1000 Keystone Industrial Park, Scranton, PA 18512.
(800) 242-7737.

THE LITTLE HOUSE SERIES:
Little House on the Prairie, Little House in the Big Woods, Farmer Boy, On the Banks of Plum Creek, By the Shores of Silver Lake, The Long Winter, Little Town on the Prairie, These Happy Golden Years and ***The First Four Years,*** all by Laura Ingalls Wilder. Grades 3-7. Published by HarperCollins Children's Books, 1000 Keystone Industrial Park, Scranton, PA 18512. (800) 242-7737.

A Little House Christmas: Holiday Stories From the Little House Books, by Laura Ingalls Wilder. Grades 3-7. Published by HarperCollins Children's Books, 1000 Keystone Industrial Park, Scranton, PA 18512. (800) 242-7737.

Reference Resources
Job Opportunities

Opportunities in Horticulture Careers, by Jan Goldberg. Grades 9 and up. Published by VGM Career Horizons, a division of NTC Publishing Group, 4255 West Touhy Ave., Lincolnwood, IL 60646.

Careers for Outdoor Types, by Andrew Kaplan. Grades 7 and up. Published by The Millbrook Press, 2 Old New Milford Rd., Brookfield, CT 06804-0335. (800) 462-4703.

Reference Resources
The Arts

The American West in the Nineteenth Century: 265 Illustrations from "Harper's Weekly" and Other Contemporary Sources, by John Grafton. Grades K-12. Published by Dover Publications, 31 East 2nd Street, Mineola, NY 11501.

Great Paintings of the Old West: In Full-Color Postcards. Grades 3-12. Published by Dover Publications, 31 East 2nd Street, Mineola, NY 11501.

Songs/Music:

Westward Ho! and ***Musical Memories of Laura Ingalls Wilder,*** book and cassette tape sets by Diane Waring. (History Alive Through Music Series). Available through Farm Country General Store, Rte. 1 Box 63, Metamora, IL 61548. (800) 551-FARM.

Photographs:

Prairie Visions: Life and Times of Solomon Butcher, by Pam Conrad. Grades 5 and up. Published by HarperCollins Children's Books, 1000 Keystone Industrial Park, Scranton, PA 18512. (800) 242-7737.

Children of the Wild West, by Russell Freedman. Grades 4-7. Published by Houghton Mifflin Co., Industrial/Trade Division, 181 Ballardvale Rd., Wilmington, MA 01887 (800) 225-3362.

Quilts:

The Quilt-Block History of Pioneer Days: With Projects Kids Can Make, by Mary Cobb. Grades 2-4. Published by The Millbrook Press, 2 Old New Milford Rd., Brookfield, CT 06804-0335. (800) 462-4703.

My Grandmother's Patchwork Quilt: A Book & Pocketful of Patchwork Pieces, by Jane Bolton. Grades 3 and up. Published by Bantam, Doubleday, Dell, Consumer Services, P.O. Box 507, Des Plains, IL 60017. (800) 223-6834. Available from Farm Country General Store, Rte. 1, Box 63, Metamora, IL 61548. (800) 551-3276.

Treasures in the Trunk: Quilts of the Oregon Trail, by Mary Cross.
Published by Rutledge Hill Press, 211 Seventh Ave. N., Nashville, TN 37212.
(800) 234-4234.

Reference Resources
Miscellaneous

The Encyclopedia of Country Living, by Carla Emery. Published by Sasquatch Books. Available from Farm Country General Store, Rte. 1, Box 63, Metamora, IL 61548. (800) 551-3276.

A Handbook of Nature Study, by Anna Comstock. Grades 5-12. Published by Cornell University Press, Sage House, 512 East State Street, Ithaca, NY 14850. Available from Greenleaf Press, 1570 Old LaGuardo Rd., Lebanon, TN 37087. (615) 449-1617.

Our National Parks, by Michael Weber. Grades 2-4. Published by The Millbrook Press, 2 Old New Milford Rd., Brookfield, CT 06804-0335. (800) 462-4703.

The Sierra Club Wayfinding Book, by Vicki McVey. Grades 5-9. Published by Sierra Club Books, Little, Brown and Co., 200 West St., Waltham, MA 02154. (800) 759-0190.

Back to Basics: How to Learn and Enjoy Traditional American Skills, published by Reader's Digest Association, Inc., Customer Service, Reader's Digest Rd., Pleasantville, NY 10570. (800) 431-1246.

Willy Whitefeather's Outdoor Survival Handbook for Kids and ***Willy Whitefeather's River Book for Kids.*** Grades 3 and up. Published by Harbinger House, P.O. Box 42948, Tucson, AZ 85733. (520) 326-9595.

Reference Resources
Science & Nature

Mammals of North America, by John Burton. (Science Nature Guides). Grades 4-9. Published by Thunder Bay Press, 5880 Oberlin Drive, Suite 400, San Diego, CA 92121.

175 Amazing Nature Experiments, by Rosie Harlow and Gareth Morgan. Grades 3-8. Published by Random House Books, 400 Hahn Rd., Westminster, MD 21157. (800) 733-3000.

One Day In The Prairie, by Jean Craighead George. Grades 3-8. Published by Thomas Y. Crowell Junior Books, 10 East 53rd Street, New York, NY 10022.

Crinkleroot's Book of Animal Tracking, Secrets of a Wildlife Watcher, Crinkleroot's Guide to Walking in Wild Places and ***Crinkleroot's Guide to Knowing the Trees,*** all by Jim Arnosky. Grades 1-4. Published by Simon & Schuster Children's Books, 200 Old Tappan Rd., Old Tappan, NJ 07675. (800) 223-2348. Available from The Elijah Company, Rte.. 2 Box 100-B, Crossville, TN 38555. (615) 456-6384.

Janice van Cleave's Machines, by Janice van Cleave. (Spectacular Science Projects Series). Grades 4 and up. Published by John Wiley & Sons, 1 Wiley Dr., Somerset, NJ 08875. (800) 225-5945.

Prairies and Grasslands, by James P. Rowan. (New True Books) Grades K-4. Published by Children's Press, P.O. Box 1331, Danbury, CT 06813. (800) 621-1115.

Tom Brown's Field Guide to Nature Observation and Survival for Children, by Tom Brown. Grades 5 and up. Published by Berkeley Publications, P.O. Box 506, East Rutherford, NJ 07073. (800) 223-0510. Available from The Elijah Company, Rte.. 2 Box 100-B, Crossville, TN 38555. (615) 456-6384.

Reading Resources

The Sign of the Beaver, by Elizabeth G. Speare. Grades 3 and up. A Dell Yearling Book, published by Bantam, Doubleday, Dell Publishing Co., P.O. Box 507, Des Plains, IL 60017. (800) 223-6834.

The Courage of Sarah Noble, by Alice Dalgliesh. Grades 1-5. Published by Aladdin Books, Simon & Schuster, owners of Macmillan Children's Books, 200 Old Tappan Rd., Old Tappan, NJ 07675-7095. (800) 223-2336.

A Gathering of Days: A New England Girl's Journal, 1830-1832, by Joan Blos. Grades 3-7. Published by Simon & Schuster, 200 Old Tappan Rd., Old Tappan, NJ 07675-7095. (800) 223-2348.

The Pioneers Go West, by George R. Stewart. Grades 5-9. (Landmark History Book). Published by Random House Books for Young Readers, 400 Hahn Rd., Westminster, MD 21157. (800) 733-3000.

Wagon Wheels, by Barbara Brenner. (Trophy I Can Read Book). Grades K-3. Published by HarperCollins Children's Books, 1000 Keystone Industrial Park, Scranton, PA 18512. (800) 242-7737.

Long Way to a New Land and ***The Long Way Westward,*** by Joan Sandin. Grades K-3. Published by HarperCollins Children's Books, 1000 Keystone Industrial Park, Scranton, PA 18512. (800) 242-7737.

The Oregon Trail, by Francis Parkman. Grades 6-12. Published by NAL-Dutton, Division of Penguin USA, 375 Hudson St., New York, NY 10014-3657. (800) 331-4624.

On To Oregon!, by Honore Morrow. Grades 4 and up. Published by Beechtree Books, William Morrow & Co., 39 Plymouth St., Fairfield, NJ 07004. (800) 843-9389.

Sarah, Plain and Tall, by Patricia MacLachlan. Grades 2-6. Published by HarperCollins Children's Books, 1000 Keystone Industrial Park, Scranton, PA 18512. (800) 242-7737.

AMERICAN GIRLS COLLECTION SERIES:
Kirsten: An American Girl, Kirsten Learns a Lesson: a School Story, Kirsten Saves the Day: A Summer Story* and *Kirsten's Surprise: A Christmas Story, all by Janet Shaw. Grades 2-6. (American Girls Collection Series). Published by Pleasant Company, P.O. Box 620190, Middleton, WI 53562-0190. (800) 845-0005.

Trouble for Lucy, by Carla Stevens. Grades 3-6. Published by Clarion Books, Houghton Mifflin Co., Individual/Trade Division, 181 Ballardvale Rd., Wilmington, MA 01887 (800) 225-3362.

Clara and the Bookwagon, by Nancy Levinson. (Trophy I Can Read Book). Grades K-3. Published by HarperCollins Children's Books, 1000 Keystone Industrial Park, Scranton, PA 18512. (800) 242-7737.

The Josefina Story Quilt, by Eleanor Coerr. (Trophy I Can Read Book). Grades K-3. Published by HarperCollins Children's Books, 1000 Keystone Industrial Park, Scranton, PA 18512. (800) 242-7737.

The Quilt Story, by Tony Johnston. Grades K-3. Published by Putnam Berkeley Group, 390 Murray Hill Parkway, East Rutherford, NJ 07073. (800) 631-8571.

San Domingo, The Medicine Hat Stallion by Marguerite Henry. Grades 3-7. Published by Aladdin, an imprint of Simon & Schuster, 200 Old Tappan Rd., Old Tappan, NJ 07675-7095. (800) 223-2336.

Justin Morgan Had a Horse, by Marguerite Henry. Grades 3-7. Published by Aladdin, an imprint of Simon & Schuster, 200 Old Tappan Rd., Old Tappan, NJ 07675-7095. (800) 223-2336.

Grasshopper Summer, by Ann Turner. Grades 3-7. Published by Simon & Schuster, 200 Old Tappan Rd., Old Tappan, NJ 07675. (800) 223-2348.

The Cabin Faced West, by Jean Fritz. (Classics Series). Grades 1-7. Published by Puffin Books, Division of Penguin USA, 375 Hudson St., New York, NY 10014. (212) 366-2000.

Diary of an Early American Boy, by Eric Sloane. Grades 3 and up. Published by Ballantine Books, subsidiary of Random House, 400 Hahn Rd., Westminster, MD 21157. (800) 726-0600.

Pioneer Bear, by Joan Sandin. (Step Into Reading Series). Grades 1-3. Published by Random House Books for Young Readers, 400 Hahn Rd., Westminster, MD 21157. (800) 733-3000.

Ox Cart Man, by Donald Hall. Grades PreK-3. Published by Puffin Books, Division of Penguin Books, 375 Hudson Street, New York, NY 10014.

My Side of the Mountain, by Jean Craig George. Grades 5-9. Published by Puffin Books, Division of Penguin USA, 375 Hudson St., New York, NY 10014. (212) 366-2000.

Caddie Woodlawn and ***Magical Melons,*** both by Carol R. Brink. Grades 4-7. Published by Simon & Schuster, 200 Old Tappan Rd., Old Tappan, NJ 07675. (800) 223-2348.

Dakota Dugout, by Ann Turner. Grades K-3. Published by Simon & Schuster, 200 Old Tappan Rd., Old Tappan, NJ 07675. (800) 223-2348.

LITTLE HOUSE SERIES:
Little House on the Prairie, Little House in the Big Woods, Farmer Boy, On the Banks of Plum Creek, By the Shores of Silver Lake, The Long Winter, Little Town on the Prairie, These Happy Golden Years and ***The First Four Years,*** all by Laura Ingalls Wilder. Grades 3-7. Published by HarperCollins Children's Books, 1000 Keystone Industrial Park, Scranton, PA 18512. (800) 242-7737.

A Little House Christmas: Holiday Stories From the Little House Books, by Laura Ingalls Wilder. Grades 3-7. Published by HarperCollins Children's Books, 1000 Keystone Industrial Park, Scranton, PA 18512. (800) 242-7737.

MY FIRST LITTLE HOUSE BOOKS SERIES:
Winter Days in the Big Woods, Dance at Grandpa's and **Going to Town,** all adapted from the Little House Books by Laura Ingalls Wilder. (My First Little House Books Series). Grades Pre-K-2. Published by HarperCollins Children's Books, 1000 Keystone Industrial Park, Scranton, PA 18512. (800) 242-7737.

The Rocky Ridge Years:
Little House On Rocky Ridge, Little Farm in the Ozarks, In the Land of the Big Red Apple and **On the Other Side of the Hill,** all by Roger Lea MacBride. Grades 3-7. Published by HarperCollins Children's Books, 1000 Keystone Industrial Park, Scranton, PA 18512. (800) 242-7737.

Eight Hands Round: A Patchwork Alphabet, by Ann W. Paul. Grades 3 and up. Published by HarperCollins Children's Books, 1000 Keystone Industrial Park, Scranton, PA 18512. (800) 242-7737.

Daniel's Duck, by Clyde Robert Bulla. (An I Can Read Book). Grades Pre-K-3. Published by Harper Trophy, 1000 Keystone Industrial Park, Scranton, PA 18512. (800) 242-7737.

Internet Resources

Here are some interesting sites on the Internet that you might want to visit while studying this unit. Please keep in mind that these pages, like all web pages, change from time to time. I recommend that you visit each site first, before the children do, to view the content and make sure that it meets your expectations. Also, use the **Subject Key Words** as search topics on Internet search engines, to find the latest additions that might pertain to this topic. (For help getting online, I highly recommend Homeschool Guide to the Online World — ISBN 1-888306-16-5.)

Daniel Boone:
http://www.berksweb.com/boone.html

Northern Prairie Science Center:
http://www.npsc.nbs.gov/

Life on the Prairie:
http://www.gps.com/life/life.htm

Stuhr Museum of the Prairie Pioneer:
http://www.classicar.com/museums/stuhr/stuhr.htm

End of the Oregon Trail:
http://www.teleport.com/%7Esligard/trail.html

Oregon Trail Wagon Train, Bayard Nebraska:
http://www.prairieweb.com/ot_wagon/otwthome.thm

The Oregon Trail:
http://www.isu.edu/~trinmich/Oregontrail.html

The Chesapeake and Ohio Canal:
http://www.fred.net/kathy/canal.html

The Appalachian Trail - State by State:
http://www.fred.net/kathy.at.atstate.html

Appalachian Trail Home Page:
http://www.fred.net/kathy/at.html

Other National Scenic Trails:
http://www.fred.net/kathy/at/scenic.html

About Murfreesboro and Rutherford County, Tennessee:
http://www.mtsu.edu/mboro/

Indian Tribes:
http://www.cs.umu.se/~dphln/wildwest/tribes.html

Girls' Series Books:
http://members.aol.com/biblioholc/gseries.html

Laura Ingalls Wilder:
tp://members.aol.com/biblioholc/Laura.html

Canyonlands National Park:
http://199.183.146.20/gorp/resource/us_national_park/ut_CANYO.HTM

Grand Canyon National Park:
http://199.183.146.20/gorp/resource/us_national_park/az_grand.htm

Ojibwe Language and Culture:
http://www.willamette.edu/~tjones/languages/ojibwe_main.html

Old Fort Museum:
http://www.fs.cei.net/museum/

About Nebraska:
http://ngp.ngpc.state.ne.us/infoeduc/usaneb.html

A Short History of Westerville:
http://www.wpl.lib.oh.us/westerville_history.html

Amanda Bennett's Unit Study Webpage:
http://www.gocin.com/unit_study/

Working Outline

I. Introduction

A. The frontier of America changed as the new country grew

    1. Initially, the frontier was whatever was "outside" the thirteen colonies

    2. As more territories were added, the frontier lines moved and changed with each addition

    3. By the end of the nineteenth century, the frontiers were closing and pioneers had settled all across the continent

B. The efforts of the pioneers helped to make America a solid and unified country

C. The lessons to be learned from a study of pioneers are many

    1. Character qualities

        a. Faith

        b. Commitment

    c. Determination

    d. Courage

    e. Love

    f. Diligence

2. Geography of the United States

3. History of the United States during the late eighteenth and nineteenth century

4. Transportation methods

5. Daily life styles and family concepts

6. Famous people involved in the pioneering efforts

7. The Indians of North America

II. History

A. Reasons for going to new territories as pioneers

    1. Adventure

    2. Privacy

    3. Fertile land

    4. Freedom

    5. Economic gain

B. Early settlers

    1. Traveled on foot or by horse

    2. Followed the trails left by animals

    3. Sought a better life and economic conditions

C. Pioneers of the nineteenth century

    1. Traveled on foot, by wagon, by boat and eventually by train

    2. Followed the new trails, carved out by animals, Native Americans, and explorers

    3. Sought more space, better land and improved economic conditions

III. Government Influence

A. The Northwest Ordinance of 1785 was passed by the Continental Congress to organize the surveying and sales of the land in the Northwest Territory (west of the original thirteen colonies, east of the Mississippi River and north of the Ohio River)

B. The Northwest Ordinance of 1787, set up the system of governing the Northwest Territory and defined the steps to statehood

C. The Constitution of the United States was signed in 1787

D. The Bill of Rights was written and became the first amendment to the Constitution in 1791

E.   The Louisiana Purchase was completed in 1803 and doubled the size of the United States

F.   In 1804, Lewis and Clark began their exploration of the west, sponsored by a $2.5 million expense budget from Congress

G.   The Preemption Act in 1841 provided for squatters to purchase the land they occupied

H.   The Homestead Act in 1862 provided for land to be obtained with the payment of a small fee and staying on the land for at least five years

IV.   Major paths of travel in the days of the early pioneers

A.   Forbes Road

B.   Braddock's Road

C.   Wilderness Trail

D.   Cumberland Road

    1.   Construction began 1811

2. Created to cross the Allegheny Mountains

3. Connected Maryland and Illinois

E. Oregon Trail

1. Originated in Missouri and ended in Oregon

2. Over 2,000 miles long

3. Followed several rivers west

4. Forts and other stops along the trail

   a. Fort Kearney

   b. Scott's Bluff

   c. Chimney Rock

   d. Fort Laramie

e.   Independence Rock

f.   Fort Bridger

g.   Fort Hall

h.   Fort Boise

i.   Whitman Mission

j.   Fort Vancouver

V.   Daily Life

A.   Life on the trail

    1.   Preparing for the journey

        a.   Planning for months in advance

        b.   Selecting what to pack and what to leave behind

c. Talking to others about any information available

2. Embarking on the long trip

    a. Goodbyes to friends and family

    b. The aches and pains of travel

    c. Finding food along the way

        (1) Supplies brought from the outset were used first

        (2) Hunting wildlife on the trail

            (a) Deer

            (b) Buffalo

            (c) Rabbit

            (d) Bear

            (e) Squirrel

            (f) Prairie Dog

            (g) Raccoon

            (h) Antelope

d.   The sights and sounds of the trip

    (1)   Landmarks

    (2)   Other travelers

    (3)   Wildlife

    (4)   Weather over the seasons of the journey

    (5)   Births, deaths and illness

e.   Stops along the way

    (1)   Sundays were days to stop, worship and rest

    (2)   River crossings

    (3)   Chimney Rock

    (4)   Independence Rock

    (5)   Forts built along the route to provide provisions and a resting place before the next part of the journey

B.   Life in the new home

    1.   Clearing the land needed for the home

    2.   Building the home

        a.   First lodging at the homesite was usually temporary (shack, shanty or dugout)

        b.   Permanent lodging was built later

            (1)   Log cabin construction if there were readily-available trees

            (2)   Sod construction if the home was built on the prairie

    3.   Daily chores

        a.   Cooking

        b.   Cleaning

        c.   Tending the livestock

        d.   Planting, tending and harvesting crops

e. Maintaining the homestead, outbuildings, and fences

f. Fetching water

g. Collecting and chopping firewood

h. Making, washing and mending clothes

i. Watching the younger children

C. Entertainment

1. Music

a. Singing of hymns, wagon train songs and classic settler songs

b. Instruments for accompaniment

(1) Fiddle

(2) Banjo

(3) Harmonica (mouth organ)

2. Social life

    a. Church or Sunday get-togethers for worship

    b. Quilting bees

    c. Corn huskings

    d. House and barn raisings

VI. Transportation

A. Walking

    1. On early trails that were too narrow for a wagon

    2. Beside the wagons along the later trails

B. Riding

    1. Horse

    2. Mule

C. Wagon

    1. Prairie schooner

    2. Conestoga wagon

D. Boat

    1. Canoe

    2. Steamboat

    3. Canal boat and barge

E. Train

VII. Famous people in the pioneering of America

A. Thomas Jefferson

B. Meriwether Lewis

C.   William Clark

D.   Sacajawea

E.   Marcus Whitman, M.D.

F.   Narcissa Whitman

G.   John Chapman (Johnny Appleseed)

H.   Kit Carson

I.   Daniel Boone

J.   Davy Crockett

K.   Zebulon Pike

L.   Buffalo Bill

M.   Jedediah Smith

VIII. North American Indians

A.   Tribal regions

1.   Northeast

2.   Southeast

3.   Plains

4.   California

5.   Basin

6.   Plateau

7.   Northwest

8.   Southwest

B.   Tribes of the Plains region of the pioneer travels

    1.   Apache

    2.   Blackfoot

    3.   Cheyenne

    4.   Comanche

    5.   Crow

    6.   Dakota

    7.   Iowa

    8.   Pawnee

    9.   Shoshoni

    10.   Sioux

C. Each tribe was unique in their beliefs and daily lives and habits

    1. Basic beliefs

    2. Daily life

        a. Family responsibilities

        b. Shelter

        c. Food

        d. Children and their roles

    3. Tribal philosophies toward the pioneers

D. Indian issues with the pioneers and American government

    1. Unkept agreements

    2. Killing and destruction of their food sources

    3. Introduction of new diseases, like measles and cholera

IX. Science in the life of the pioneers

A. Survival skills

    1. Ability to find food

    2. Ability to find water

    3. Maintain good health

    4. Care for those afflicted with illness or wounds

B. Tracking and observation skills

    1. To find food

    2. To follow the trail of others

C. Wayfinding skills

    1. Knowledge of the anticipated trail

    2. Ability to determine direction using the sun and moon and stars

3. Observing nature for other obvious directions

D. Inventions that impacted the pioneering efforts

1. Barbed wire

2. Telegraph

3. Photography

4. Improved farming tools

X. Classic literature

A. *The Little House Series* of books by Laura Ingalls Wilder

B. *The Adventures of Tom Sawyer* and *The Adventures of Huckleberry Finn* by Mark Twain (Samuel Clemens)

C. *The Oregon Trail* by Francis Parkman

D. *The Last of the Mohicans* by James Fenimore Cooper

About The Author

Amanda Bennett, author and speaker, wife and mother of three, holds a degree in mechanical engineering. She has written this ever-growing series of unit studies for her own children, to capture their enthusiasm and nurture their gifts and talents. The concept of a thematic approach to learning is a simple one. Amanda will share this simplification through her books, allowing others to use these unit study guides to discover the amazing world that God has created for us all.

Science can be a very intimidating subject to teach, and Amanda has written this series to include science with other important areas of curriculum that apply naturally to each topic. The guides allow more time to be spent enjoying the unit study, instead of spending weeks of research time to prepare for each unit. She has shared the results of her research in the guides, including plenty of resources for areas of the study, spelling and vocabulary lists, fiction and nonfiction titles, possible careers within the topic, writing ideas, activity suggestions, addresses of manufacturers, teams, and other helpful resources.

The science-based series of guides currently includes the Unit Study Adventures titles:

Baseball	Homes
Computers	Oceans
Elections	Olympics
Electricity	Pioneers
Flight	Space
Gardens	Trains

The holiday-based series of guides currently includes the Unit Study Adventures titles:

Christmas
Thanksgiving

This planned 40-book series will soon include additional titles, which will be released periodically. We appreciate your interest. "Enjoy the Adventure."